The Eyes Have It

The Story of Lashes, Looks and My Love for Them

Elizabeth Jennings

ROYSTON
Publishing

BK Royston Publishing
P. O. Box 4321
Jeffersonville, IN 47131
502-802-5385
http://www.bkroystonpublishing.com
bkroystonpublishing@gmail.com

© Copyright – 2017

All Rights Reserved. No part of this book may be reproduced, stored in a retrieval system, or transmitted by any means without the written permission of the author.

Cover Design: Jayson Saludo
Professional photo credits: Guenter Weber (G.W. Photography and Frank Haeussler

ISBN: 978-1-946111-39-5

Printed in the United States of America

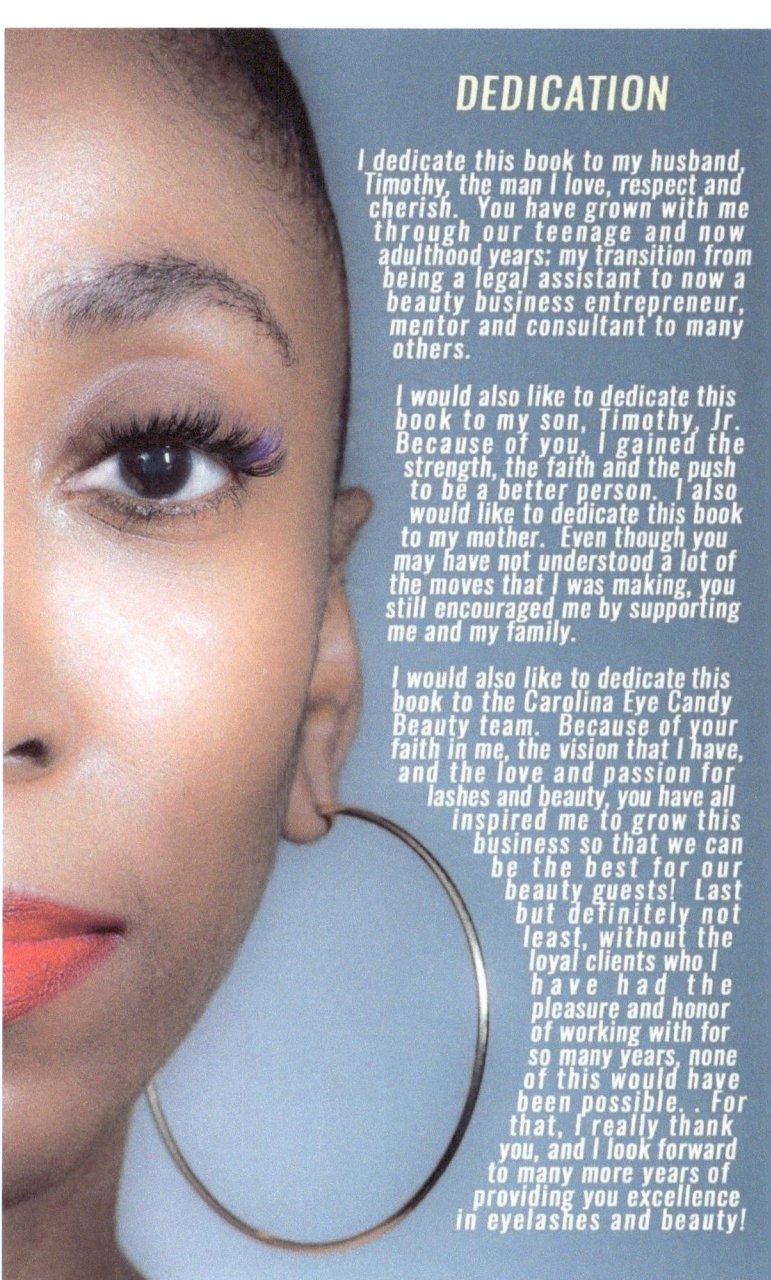

DEDICATION

I dedicate this book to my husband, Timothy, the man I love, respect and cherish. You have grown with me through our teenage and now adulthood years; my transition from being a legal assistant to now a beauty business entrepreneur, mentor and consultant to many others.

I would also like to dedicate this book to my son, Timothy, Jr. Because of you, I gained the strength, the faith and the push to be a better person. I also would like to dedicate this book to my mother. Even though you may have not understood a lot of the moves that I was making, you still encouraged me by supporting me and my family.

I would also like to dedicate this book to the Carolina Eye Candy Beauty team. Because of your faith in me, the vision that I have, and the love and passion for lashes and beauty, you have all inspired me to grow this business so that we can be the best for our beauty guests! Last but definitely not least, without the loyal clients who I have had the pleasure and honor of working with for so many years, none of this would have been possible. . For that, I really thank you, and I look forward to many more years of providing you excellence in eyelashes and beauty!

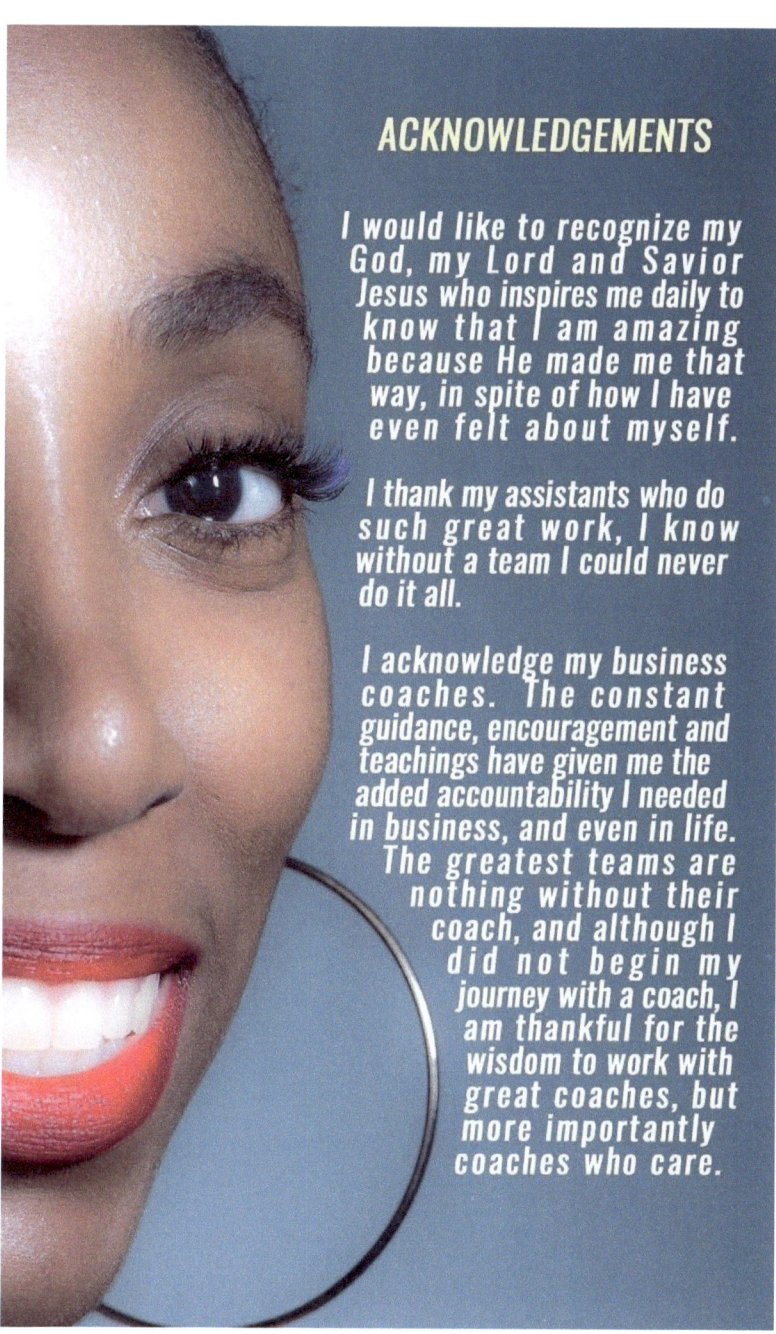

ACKNOWLEDGEMENTS

I would like to recognize my God, my Lord and Savior Jesus who inspires me daily to know that I am amazing because He made me that way, in spite of how I have even felt about myself.

I thank my assistants who do such great work, I know without a team I could never do it all.

I acknowledge my business coaches. The constant guidance, encouragement and teachings have given me the added accountability I needed in business, and even in life. The greatest teams are nothing without their coach, and although I did not begin my journey with a coach, I am thankful for the wisdom to work with great coaches, but more importantly coaches who care.

Table of Contents

Dedication	iii
Acknowledgements	v
Introduction	ix
Eyelash Chronicles	1
Could This Be Love? My Passion for Lashes and What They Do	7
Eyelash Strips - Not just for Snuffleupagus Anymore	27
Cluster Lashes - The "Knockoff" Individual Eyelash	37
Single Strand Eyelash Extensions - The True Individual Extension	49
Russian Volume Lashes - The Answer to Our Voluminous Prayers	65

From Subtle to Sexy - Why A "Little" is Never Enough   77

It's Not For Everyone, But For the Majority… Lashes RULE!!!   85

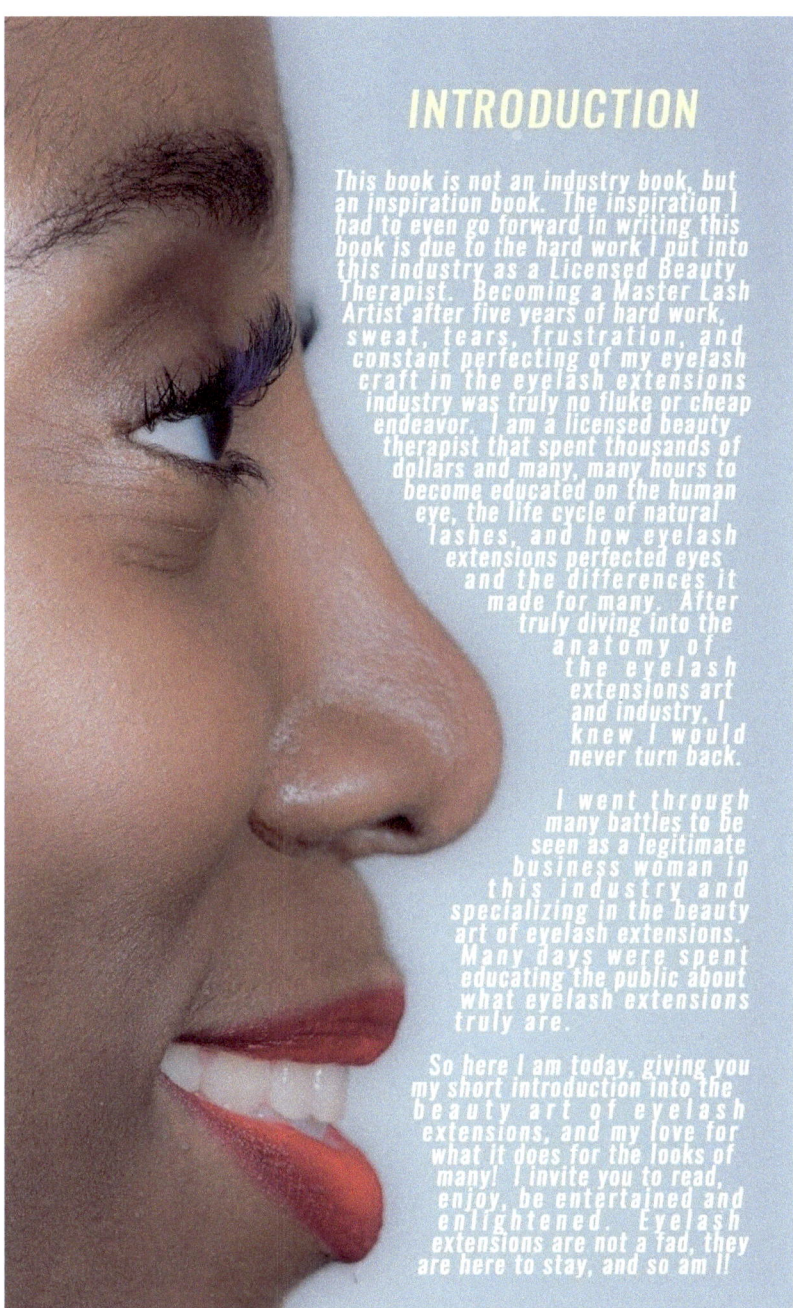

INTRODUCTION

This book is not an industry book, but an inspiration book. The inspiration I had to even go forward in writing this book is due to the hard work I put into this industry as a Licensed Beauty Therapist. Becoming a Master Lash Artist after five years of hard work, sweat, tears, frustration, and constant perfecting of my eyelash craft in the eyelash extensions industry was truly no fluke or cheap endeavor. I am a licensed beauty therapist that spent thousands of dollars and many, many hours to become educated on the human eye, the life cycle of natural lashes, and how eyelash extensions perfected eyes and the differences it made for many. After truly diving into the anatomy of the eyelash extensions art and industry, I knew I would never turn back.

I went through many battles to be seen as a legitimate business woman in this industry and specializing in the beauty art of eyelash extensions. Many days were spent educating the public about what eyelash extensions truly are.

So here I am today, giving you my short introduction into the beauty art of eyelash extensions, and my love for what it does for the looks of many! I invite you to read, enjoy, be entertained and enlightened. Eyelash extensions are not a fad, they are here to stay, and so am I!

The Eyes Have It

The Eyes Have It

Chapter 1

Eyelash Chronicles

Are your eyelashes too short? Are you jealous when you see girls with long eyelashes? Do you know that fake eyelashes, eyelash extensions and eyelash mascara were invented and further developed for the people who want luscious eyelashes? Did you ever wonder how it all started?

Well guess what? Cleopatra probably had faux eyelashes. And if she did, I can understand why she was regarded as one of the most beautiful and powerful women in history! The use of green and black color ointments applied by both men and women to their eyelashes and lids, can be traced back as early as 3500 BC in Egypt.

Ancient Romans followed suit by mixing kohl, burnt cork and saffron or antimony to make their lashes look thick and dark. It seemed that Romans found long, curled and thick eyelashes to be a trait most sought-after. That was in 753-625 BC! Amazing isn't it?!

Elizabeth Jennings

It doesn't end there though. Starting in the Middle Ages, women started experimenting with their fashion styles regarding their eyes, eyelashes and even eyebrows. From 476-1450, women in Europe started removing their eyelashes and eyebrows just to make their foreheads look elongated.

Guess we may not know exactly why they did that, as each season in time has its trends that may not make sense to others later. But could you still imagine how painful that is? And to think they were plucking those brows and lashes the old fashioned way.

Starting from the reign of Queen Elizabeth I (I like to imagine sometimes I'm from royalty with the name Elizabeth. I was named after my grandmother and mother for their middle names. But Hey! I can definitely imagine myself being royalty LOL) from the year 1533-1603, who had natural reddish-gold colored locks, women try and are still imitating Her Highness. In the Elizabethan Era, they would dye both their brows and eyelashes in different tones of red; however, they were proven to be very dangerous. Women who secretly dyed their lashes in private using soot from fireplaces and crushed berries often experienced hair loss because of some toxic substances used. The first commercial and non-toxic mascara was introduced during the Victorian Era, considered as the Roman-

tic Era. A perfumer for Queen Victoria; Eugene Rimmel, introduced the mascara (a small wand resembling a mini comb) in 1840. He used Vaseline Jelly and coal dust to create what the people at that time found to be sensational.

Eyelashes and Their Evolution Over the Years

In order to help actress Seena Owen have larger and more prominent eyelashes; D.W. Griffith, the American film director of the 1916 epic "Intolerance," first invented the false eyelashes. Human haïr was woven to fine gauze before attaching it to the actress' lids with gum.

Elizabeth Jennings

It became popular in the early 1930's. Maybelline first

started their mascara when a woman in 1917 named Maybel Williams sought help from a drug manufacturer to create a sheen formula using oil and petroleum jelly. They called it, 'Lash-Brow-Ine.' The Maybelline mascara was then trademarked in 1920 by Tom Lyle Williams. We now know how the famous Maybelline brand began. The next year, Charles Nessler filed the US patent for 'Artificial Eyelashes and Ways of Making the Same.'

The patent was released in 1923. That same year, William Beldue invented the very first eyelash curler, calling it 'Kurlash.' It is modelled from scissors and made of stainless-steel. Helene Vierhaler patented waterproof mascara in 1938.

From there, various kinds of mascara were introduced. From Revlon's Roll-on mascara in 1958 to Yardley's Twiggy Lashes in 1967, women were exposed to an almost stream of products to help enhance lashes.

The Eyes Have It

Various colors of mascara were also launched in 1961. Maybelline launched Great Lash Mascara while Arnold and Sydell Miller founded Ardell Lashes in 1971.

Eyelashes at Present

Existing companies and newly founded ones continue to introduce different products for eyelashes. In 1984, Lin McKinstry established MEI-CHA and extended it a year later. Eyelash extensions were first introduced in the US in 2004 and in 2008, Latisse was approved by FDA for treatment of inadequate lashes. The main ingredient in Latisse; Bimatoprost, is the main ingredient in glaucoma medications to control the pressure of the eyes. One of the side effects was it caused many patients' eyelashes to grow! So someone decided to get that patented, and voila! Another beauty enhancement product on the market, but with a prescription only.

Elizabeth Jennings

Eyelashes and the history of eyelashes have evolved as years passed by. The steady evolution of lashes and the constant enhancement makes one wonder how the evolvement will continue.

Chapter 2

"Could This Be Love? My Passion for Lashes and What They Do For Looks!"

My History and Love for Lashes

Every day I am able to do a set of eyelash extensions, I am in heaven! I never realized the importance of eyelashes for one's appearance before providing this service myself. When eyelashes are enhanced, they're not only giving one the appearance of fuller lashes but it gives one an awakening and vibrancy. And let's face it, lashes give life! I feel this way when I get my lashes done for sure, but my beauty guests say it all the time. I can quote many when they have said, "I feel alive again!" "I'm back!"

Eyelashes also help to lift up one's eyes to make them appear more youthful; no matter what their age! Let's face it! There are so many types of eyes and definitely some eye 'issues.' Whether the eyes have hooded eyelids, heavy drooping skin, discolored eyelids and etc, eyelash extensions are an awesome camouflage for these 'issues.' When I completed my first eyelash extensions training in 1998, I honestly felt like I was in a daze and maybe also a bit confused. Seeing as I was one that was coming from a different type of professional field; being a legal assistant, and then transitioning to being a licensed massage therapist, working in the medical field and then also in the spa atmospheres, this was an extreme change for me.

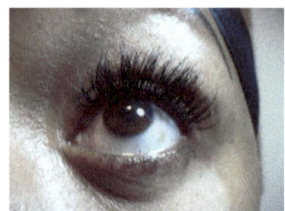

Being in an eyelash extensions training class felt a bit foreign to me. I knew that being a Licensed Massage Therapist meant that I was qualified to take the training, but I didn't feel the sense of confidence that I needed to really think the training was for me. I knew I wanted to do something that would be able to enhance one's looks and give them that "WOW" factor. I knew that I did not want to be a cosmetologist and do hair services. That was just not my thing!

The Eyes Have It

So being in this training class, and seeing these incredibly small synthetic eyelashes and then seeing these sharp instruments that I was going to be using to place eyelash extensions on someone's eyes, made me feel both a bit perplexed and nervous. I was ready to start my new endeavor of eyelash extensions, because the training had more than prepared me for the process of getting started.

Overcoming my fear was imperative. I started feeling confident after picking up the tweezers and practicing applying extensions on practice strips of lashes. I then had to practice on a physical model in the class. Even though I was nervous; I was extremely excited. Excited about WHAT you may ask?

I was excited about my future, where this could take me and what I was going to be able to do for others. I felt like I was finally beginning the path of allowing a woman to have something that they didn't have before they came to see me. What I was doing was enhancing their eyes.

I was going to be able to participate in that "before and after" journey that so many women I had encountered in the salon and spa industry. Also what they were receiving at the hands of other talented hair stylists and beauty artists that I had the privilege of working with. I so desperately wanted to be a part of that! Don't get me wrong. Being a licensed massage therapist, and providing stress and pain relief, along with relaxation was profound. I enjoyed every bit of that, but I also desired more instant gratification.

No, I wasn't doing a cut and color on a woman's hair. No, I wasn't doing a funky set of nails which had beautiful colors, crystals and designs on them. I was giving someone something that they didn't have before which was longer and fuller lashes! (And what could be better than that, am I right?) This was something that was really new to me, but I was just really so excited to just get these lashes on that model and see the "after" effect.

The Eyes Have It

So when I was finished performing the service for the first time on my model, I removed the eyelash coverings from her lower lashes so she could open her eyes and look in the mirror. I was in awe (just like the model was in awe) of what we were seeing. (That would be me and my instructor of course, ha ha!) The look of Bambi-like eyes  and flirty lashes was amazing! That service was the moment that I found my passion for lashes and the ability of lashes to change one's entire look!

So from that very moment I knew I had to continue doing this, and I wanted to put lashes on as many people as possible. I would have put them on my puppy, if my puppy would have allowed me to do so at the time. I just really wanted to place eyelashes on everyone. (OK, that clearly was a joke, but you get my drift, I was just excited!) Within two years after my initial training, I had placed eyelashes on a variety of people. My calendar was constantly booked with appointments. I had worked on so many different sets of eyes. I have placed eyelash extensions on Caucasian women, African-American women, Hispanic women, Asian women. I have even put eyelash extensions on males. No matter who I worked with; whatever race, ethnicity or their age, it did not matter. Every time I did a set of lashes, it was as if I have done them for the first time. When I was able to give the beauty guest that mirror so that they could look at their enhanced eyelashes, it was a moment of amazement!

Being able to hear a beauty guest share their satisfaction, watch them look in the mirror after having a beautiful full set of eyelash extensions applied to their eyes and hear them say, "WOW" or "Oh My God," it just always does something for me. I never get tired of hearing that! It allows me to know that the passion that I have for this service is the same passion that they have for being their best selves and making that investment in themselves to enhance their looks by enhancing their eyes.

The Eyes Have It

Different People, Different Lashes

When a beauty guest (female or male) has lashes which are straight and they're looking for more of a curl than they naturally have, this beauty service allows me to give them a lasting curl. These beautiful extensions; which can be either a nice natural curl or a tighter more exaggerate curl, are going to give them that lift that they're looking for so their eyes are enhanced naturally. It's so refreshing!

When a beauty guest has lashes which point downward, I tend to go for a more dramatic look by giving them the tightest curl on their extensions so they have a more drastic effect. When one has downward pointing lashes, it can make them look sad. This type of eyelash also tends to make them look tired, and sometimes they feel how they look just by default. So giving someone lashes can change both their look and how they feel.

Elizabeth Jennings

I have worked with a lot of women who have really curly natural lashes, but the lashes go haywire and the lashes go in all different directions. So their lashes are not necessarily straight or downward pointing lashes like some people have. When someone has lashes that are "untamable," then having the ability to apply eyelash extensions to those eyes gives their lashes a more uniform appearance. Those curly, messy lashes tend to blend in more, and I can hide those imperfections when I am able to apply a nice full set of eyelash extensions to those natural lashes which go haywire. These types of natural lashes; I must admit are not the easiest to work with, but I deal with it like a champ. What I mean by that is that, Yes, it is a challenge, but I am up for it. I conquer those lashes by taking my time, concentrating and individually isolating those lashes that tend to kink, twist and curl. Those lashes take more time to work with. Sometimes I may pop a few beads of sweat, but the outcome is absolutely worth it.

My favorite lashes to apply for someone who has

messy, naturally curly lashes or just naturally haywire lashes is the: 'Russian Volume Lashes.' The Russian Volume Lashes (or the Ru-Vol-ution as I and many lash artists like to call it) allow me as a Master Lash Artist to give that beauty guest more definition and more density. It's really going to help to hide those lashes and hide any areas where there are gaps or spaces in their natural eyelash line. Even though I have been applying professional eyelash extensions since 2008, I still sometimes get a little bit of anxiety when I have a new beauty guest who comes in with lashes that are like this kind. Because I am in such a state of focus and calm when I am doing eyelash extensions, it does not bother me. I just want to make sure that I am giving that beauty guest the best that I've got.

When I'm performing a set of eyelash extensions, I'm really in my Zen zone. I don't feel any anxiety...I don't feel frustrated...I don't feel like I wish this was over... It is a very tedious process, but I am in my comfort zone when I am providing a beauty guest with a full set of eyelash extensions or providing a maintenance fill in. Sometimes beauty guests will fall asleep when I'm providing the service, but that is an honor for me! Why? Simply because it lets me know that they are really relaxed, and that helps me to be even more in a state of Zen and calm when I'm providing the service. The rest or "beauty sleep" that they are able to enjoy while lying on the treatment table while the service is being performed, is also amazing for their looks as well. It helps their eyes to be more well rested, and the perfection that I am giving them culminates together!

When the beauty guest has eyes that tend to droop on the outer corners or "downward pointing eyes," it is amazing how I can transform the look of their eyes by simply applying a really nice exaggerated curl of lashes to their mid to outer corner of the eyes. Those simple extensions will completely give the eyes a nice lift! I wouldn't have it any other way. Eyelash extensions also give a lot of women the confidence to go without wearing makeup, because their eyes are already mostly made-up and ready for the day. They're able to get rid of that mascara, and just wake up looking refreshed of course after cleansing their face. To be able to forego a lot of makeup is wonderful for a woman's looks, because the less you are applying makeup every day, the more you are allowing your skin to breathe! It also reduces the chances of breakouts due to the clogging of the pores, because of all the makeup that's being applied on a regular basis. It's a definite "win-win."

I've had so many women over the years tell me how they just get up and go. They put on their lip color if they're going to wear it, and they may fill in their brows and they're finished. They don't have to put on mascara, eyeliner or eyeshadow, and they can eliminate all of these different makeup rituals that some people do on a regular basis. I would also say that it's probably saved a lot of lives on the road, because they don't have to put on mascara while they're driving to work anymore. That's always a plus. #livessaved

Elizabeth Jennings

Sometimes it happens literally overnight. A woman of a certain age looks in the mirror, and realizes how much has changed over the years since they were in their younger years and they had more lashes to work with. They begin to research and learn about what we are able to do for them. I have to say this is one of the best feelings for me! A beauty guest who does their research and finds my company because of my reputation is definitely a thrill! I know they know their stuff, and they believe we are the right people for the job after doing that research! When I'm able to apply lashes to a woman whose natural lashes have diminished over time and they're a lot thinner and sparser and finer than they used to be, the fact that I'm able to apply some lashes to their eyes means that I've rejuvenated their appearance in a magnificent way. This gives both my beauty client and myself a great feeling of accomplishment. I like to say I perform miracles with eyelashes, and I truly believe that I do! (I just don't have a magic wand, but maybe my eyelash tweezers are like mini magic wands? Food for thought! Hmm . . . .) I've had women look in the mirror after getting their lashes done for the first time and have turned around and given me a huge hug, because I made such a difference in their life. That is what gives me the passion to keep going and finding those that I need to help and can help.

I have an amazing beauty guest that I have been working with for several years now, and the first time I ever saw her was due to a natural lash trauma that she experienced. She used to curl her natural lashes with an eyelash curler and apply mascara. Using an eyelash curler periodically may be okay, but when you're using it on a rather frequent basis it causes tension to your natural lashes. You can be loosening the lashes from the follicles and then eventually causing them to rip out. That is known as 'Tension Alopecia.' The same thing happens with the hairs on your head, if you are continually putting them in styles where your hair strands are being pulled rather hard often.

Over time, your hair starts to recede and may fall out; sometimes not growing back. Unfortunately, this is what happened with her lashes. When she came to my business, she was desperate for assistance with her lashes due to 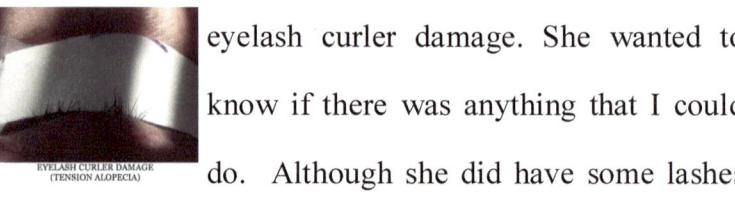 eyelash curler damage. She wanted to know if there was anything that I could do. Although she did have some lashes remaining, she did not have a lot. She also had a lot of gaps and spaces in her lash bed. What we needed to do to camouflage that, was to apply some lashes to the lash follicle area for a temporary basis just to make sure she was not walking around and looking like she completely had no lashes.

So even though it was something that was not typical for me to do, it was something that I had to do for her. I could not turn her away and say, "I'm sorry, there's nothing that I can do for you." I recommended an eyelash serum which would condition her follicles and strengthen the base of her lashes.

The Eyes Have It

This serum would also help her lashes grow back at a faster rate. So once we did that for a period, of four to six weeks with the eyelash serums and also applying some temporary lashes to her eyes for about two appointment cycles, her lashes were growing back in full.

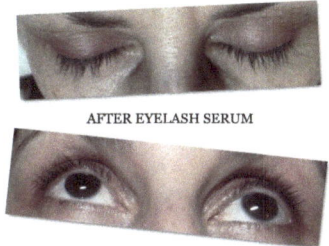
AFTER EYELASH SERUM

Then it was time to really get into the business of lashing! Although in my mind I was thinking, 'She probably just wanted to get this temporary lash fix until her natural lashes grew back; thereafter, maybe she would just continue to use the eyelash serum and go back to wearing mascara. She then realized how much eyelashes did for her looks and how much time it saved her daily; she decided. Having your hair strands being pulled rather hard, often and over time, your hair starts to recede and may fall out; sometimes not growing back. Unfortunately this is what happened with her lashes. When she came to my business, she was desperate. She wanted to know if there was anything that I could do.

Elizabeth Jennings

Although she did have some lashes remaining, she did not have a lot. She also had spaces and broken off lashes in her lash bed, I recommended an eyelash serum and conditioner to help strengthen her lashes at the follicle level, and help her natural lashes to grow back thicker

AFTER VOLUME LASHES
"THE UPGRADE 👄"

and stronger. I also recommended we apply some temporary lashes to camouflage the damage. This was a bit unconventional, because the entire process of applying eyelash extensions is to apply them to natural lashes. She clearly had some areas where there were no lashes, or they were extremely short. Because she is a professional woman, she decided to continue to have her lashes enhanced to save time and skip the eyelash curling and mascara ritual she was so used to for many years. The temporary lashes were okay, but she took my professional advice to step it up and go with an upgrade of a lash service that was more visually appealing than what she received for a temporary fix.

The Eyes Have It

So we went for the gusto and we went for the Volume Lashes; (2D Volume Lashes to be exact). It was a huge win for me too, because I was able to give her something that she never even imagined before. She now has an intensifying lash look with her eyelash extensions and does not have to put on mascara every day. This was a huge accomplishment for me that I was able to give her what she was looking for in an emergency situation. I then helped her to realize that wearing eyelashes on a regular basis was a huge win for her in terms of saving her time in her day, saving a step and just always getting compliments on her eyes and her lashes. Now when people ask her what type of mascara she is wearing, she can proudly say that she's not wearing any!

The passion that I have for lashes just really fuels my drive for wanting to help so many women. In my career thus far, I have literally worked with thousands of women pairing the best- in-style looks for their circumstances and situations when it involves the service of eyelash extensions.

I'm extremely thankful, blessed and excited about that. When I sit and say that I have worked with thousands of women sometimes, I can't even believe that has actually happened, but it really has.

There are so many different types of eye shapes, and so many different eyelash styles. Some people have always had naturally thin lashes, and some people have naturally dense lashes with so many lashes as far as the eye could see. I always say that I believe it was God's sense of humor that most boys and men have naturally amazing eyelashes which are full, thick and long. While women who may have had naturally dense and voluminous lashes when they were younger, soon realize that their lashes are not as dense and full as they grow older.

Then some women have never had naturally dense and voluminous lashes, so they've always needed some enhancement. It's crazy to think about, but it's actually true.

The Eyes Have It

As we age, we start to lose hair in the places that we really want it, and gain it in the areas where we really don't need it! But I love being able to add eyelashes to our beauty guests' eyes to give them what they naturally don't have occurring. It is both a game changer and a face changer. I wouldn't have it any other way.

Chapter 3

Eyelash Strips - Not just for Snuffleupagus

Anymore Mr. Snuffleupagus, Anyone?

Do you remember that Sesame street character Snuffleupagus? I think we all do as children. When someone mentions that Sesame Street character, the first thing that you can think of, is NOT the fact that it is a big fuzzy elephant. The VERY thing that most people remember is the very long eyelashes that this elephant was "blessed" with!. In the days and times that we are in, we have seen a lot of women that are wearing eyelash strips.

Eyelash strips have been around for many, many years. Eyelash strips are a great option and it's not for everyone, but it definitely can serve its purpose if worn correctly. There are literally thousands of different types of eyelash strips that are available today. Eyelash strips continue to evolve as technology evolves. They come in different lengths, curls and materials, and there are some decorative types that even have crystals, feathers and other embellishments.

Eyelash strips definitely are one of those things that are perfect for parties when you really want to give your eyes a dramatic look. It's great as well for costuming (especially for Halloween). Eyelash strips are being used more in these days by those who are not in the market; budget wise, to be able to afford something that is done on a more frequent basis.

These products are made to be worn and removed every single day. That is one of the downsides of eyelash strips. They are not very easy to put on. When most people who wear them on a regular basis wear them, they don't want to do it every single day, so they're looking for a way to be able to wear them at night and wake up and still have them on.

The Eyes Have It

Eyelash Strips and Hair Extensions

Eyelash strips are similar to hair extensions in the sense that you have a weft of either human hair or synthetic fibers that are woven onto creating a seam where all of the lashes are inter-twined or interconnected. Then this strip is where the glue is applied to place on the eyelash line. Most glues that are used for eyelash strips are 100% safe and water soluble. Some are made of latex, so someone who has an allergy to latex products would want to ensure that they are using an eyelash strip product that is not going to contain any latex. They would want to ensure that they are not using any eyelash glue that has any latex in it, because it could cause an allergic reaction.

This really is a great commodity, but it has gotten a bad reputation. There have been so many circumstances where women went to places that are not licensed to do an eyelash service. They are having these really thick, heavy eyelash strips glued on to their eyes using bonding glue that are made for hair extensions (or other purposes).

When services are not done in a proper way and the products isn't used in the way it was intended to, it really gives the product and the service provider a bad look! So a lot of people have really been hard on women that wear eyelash strips, because they have been wearing them so thick and heavy and with visible "clumpy" glue! If this product is used the proper way and worn the proper way, there really wouldn't be this epidemic of people going around looking like Snuffleupagus! (But let's be honest! Not even Snuffle looked as bad as some of the looks I've seen!) So saying that eyelash strips are not for Snuffleupagus anymore, is really my attempt to let people know and educate them that there are great eyelash strips which can be worn. If you are educated in the proper way to wear the extensions, you can obtain a great look for any beauty addict.

BAD WAY OF WEARING EYELASH STRIPS

The Eyes Have It

The Importance of Using Eyelash Strips Properly

I'll give a great example of a time when eyelash strips were just what the doctor ordered. (Call me the Eyelash Doctor!) We had a potential beauty guest and this person was a minor so their mother actually called in to say that their daughter was having issues with their eyes, was losing her eyelash hair and she didn't know what was going on! She was really freaked out about this. I guess I would be too if I had a daughter that was in that age group where all the girls in school cared about their looks. I asked this mother if her daughter had been diagnosed with '*alopecia.*' She said that she had not been, but she also felt that she was pulling her eyelashes out so she wanted to know if she could get eyelash extensions done and if it would help her daughter not to do that anymore. Her daughter was not diagnosed with this, but 'Trichotillomania' which is a condition where one pulls their hair out consistently. It is a nervous condition; and although rare, it does exist.

Elizabeth Jennings

I told her that it would not help the issue, but if she wanted to do something so that her eyes wouldn't look completely bald we may be able to do an alternative service. So I asked if she could just bring her daughter in for an eyelashes consultation. We could look at her eyes and her lashes; whatever was left of them, and go from there. She brought her daughter in, and she was not exaggerating. Her daughter literally had no lashes except a few stubs, and you could see the breakage so there definitely was some pulling. The lashes that were left were extremely short with blunt edges. Blunt edges on the lashes indicate the clipping, cutting, pulling or snapping of those lashes.

So what I recommended for her daughter was to use an extremely natural looking eyelash strip, and she agreed. So we used products that were not going to damage her eyes or harm her eyes in anyway. This was going to give her daughter a nice, clean, natural clean look. We performed the eyelash strip service, with my direction and by the hands of my senior Lash Stylist; Alisha. First and foremost, we cleansed her eye area where her lashes were and where they used to be. Then we applied; using eyelash strip glue, a very natural, thin eyelash strip to her eye area. To the lashes on the eyelash strip, we added temporary eyelash enhancements to those, to provide a very natural but fun look for the young lady. Her mother was in awe and appreciative for what we did for her daughter and her daughter felt the same way! At that moment, that really did something for me because it helped me to realize how important a job I really have. **It's not just about vanity and about feeding into someone's ego, but about how important their looks are.** This is about how people feel better about themselves, and that is an amazing opportunity to help others.

But while I am opening up, I'll be quite honest with you. I'm a bit of a lash snob. What that means is that when I think about eyelashes, I think about the natural, individual lashes that one can have. So if I have to choose between eyelash strips and eyelash extensions, it would be eyelash extensions all the way for me baby! There has been so much uproar in the lash beauty community about eyelash strips, and how they damage lashes and all these different things. So I felt the need to educate people about eyelash strips and let them know that it's not the eyelash strips that damages one's lashes, but how they were worn, how they were applied and even who's applying them. I wanted everyone who desired eyelash extensions to be able to have them-for whatever reason, either budgetary or just because they don't have the full natural lashes that they have always wanted.

I created a line of eyelash strips that are really great and natural looking, and in different personality styles depending on the person wearing them. I have them in mink and in human hair options, so that they have a natural feel and a natural appearance.

The Eyes Have It

There are lots of synthetic eyelash strips, but they tend to look shiny and fake and no one would ever believe they are natural lashes.

Most people wouldn't want to call attention to their eyes, so wearing something as natural as possible is something right up their alley. I wanted to be able to serve those people.

I'm not here to change the eyelash strips game, I am just here to change a few of the rules that were applied. As I've said before, "I'm an 'eyelash snob' and at times, seeing such awful examples of lashes can be almost painful." It has been a practice in restraint that I have had to start applying; not to have a reaction of shock or discomfort on my face, when I see these women with heavy duty eyelash strips that look dirty and look like they have a lot of old "clumpy" glue on them or falling off their eyes.

Elizabeth Jennings

It just doesn't have to be that way, so creating something that can be worn by the everyday woman or by someone who is a professional in any industry is an amazing thing. I am happy to be able to do this.

So move over Snuffleupagus lashes, and make room for Tempting Lashes (™).

The Eyes Have It

Chapter 4

Cluster Lashes - The "Knockoff" Individual Eyelash

When I began doing eyelash extensions in 2008, it was really a challenge getting the message out about what eyelash extensions really were. In my community, there are eyelash services being done but it really wasn't what I wanted to do for people. I wanted to offer quality services, and I wanted to offer natural eyelashes that enhance a woman's eyes and not drastically change their looks.

Cluster lashes are cool, but I believe that they are there for a certain purpose as well. Cluster lashes are made of a synthetic fiber (6-8 strands), which are then tied on the end to create a knot (or cluster). They're also made in knot-free option as well, but these lashes are made for temporary use and not long term wear. Cluster lashes are great for just applying for a dramatic eye look for a party, a Photo shoot or for an event, but I don't believe that they are made for everyday wear.

Elizabeth Jennings

When I started doing eyelash extensions, I had an uphill battle. There were so many people that I encountered that would say, "Oh I've gotten individual eyelashes before," but then I would find that they were talking about cluster eyelashes and not true individual eyelash extensions.

You see. Differentiating cluster lashes from an eyelash strip; you may call it an individual, because it's not one full strip that's being applied to the eye. Indeed a cluster lash is not an individual eyelash extension, but it is a cluster of lashes to create a fuller look for a period of time. For cluster lashes to be worn the right way, you would use the same type of glue that you would use for eyelash strips. The type of glue that you would use for cluster eyelashes would be either be a latex based or latex free glue that is water resistant. There had been an epidemic of women getting these "individual lashes" applied to their natural lashes on their eyes.

The Eyes Have It

These cluster lashes were sometimes applied in a way that they are damaging to their eyes. You see these cluster lashes are being applied and made to be really

CLUSTER LASHES GONE WRONG 😖
NOT MY WORK 🌸

thick and heavy. A huge issue with this is that the 'service providers' that were providing the lash service were using adhesives not meant to be applied on a beauty guest's eye area. Same issue was with the strip eyelashes, with having people that were not licensed to do any Aesthetics services such as a nail technician, using nail glue or sometimes even nail bonding glue for hair extensions to place these lashes on people's eyes. This is not a 'knock' on nail techs, but in the state I reside, I am licensed to work. Nail technicians are only licensed to provide nail services; not aesthetics services in which eyelash extensions fall in the category of esthetics. I have seen so many instances of women coming into my beauty business to have their eyes examined or to have the lashes removed.

Elizabeth Jennings
Why You Should Go To An Expert

I can remember several years ago, there was a woman that went to a nail salon locally and she had cluster lashes applied to her eyes. She called my salon to see if she could
have them removed. Honestly, I wasn't sure if I wanted to do it, because we didn't apply these lashes to her eyes. In my professional opinion, it would have been best to go back to the place where she got those lashes and have them removed there. The reason she did not go back to this place to have them removed was, because they were being extremely difficult with her.

She was having issues with her eyes, and she said that the process took very long and that she was sitting up in either a stool or a chair while the service was being done. That alone is a red light in my professional opinion, because she said she was experiencing some pain while it was being done. She was sitting up in a chair or in a stool in an open area where nail services were being done.

The Eyes Have It

So, it wasn't even done in a way that was discreet or in a way that was professional. In a nail salon where acetone is being used and fumes are abundant, a client should not be having work done on her eyes. When you walk into nail salon, the first thing you smell is usually not the smell of roses, is it?

In the State of South Carolina, aesthetics services are only supposed to be done by licensed esthetician; which is what I am, or licensed cosmetologists. It's not uncommon practice for a licensed cosmetologist to work in a nail salon doing nail services, but it is highly unlikely that a person that is providing these services were licensed cosmetologists. When she called them back to let them know that she was still having some issues, her eyes were in pain and she needed to have these lashes removed. She said that they were really being difficult with her. She wanted to come in to have these lashes removed, but she also wanted to know what type of glue was being used on her eyes. She said they refused to tell her what they used, they refused to remove the lashes and told her to just put some oil on her eyes and the lashes will just come off. Very unprofessional!

So because I just really felt bad for her, I had her come in. I was booked that day, but I had one of my team members remove the lashes for her; it was a hard task. We have had to remove eyelashes before for a beauty guest that was someone we had applied eyelash extensions for various reasons. They were moving away, and they did not want to try to find someone that did lashes in the area, or that they just wanted to give their eyes a break for the season or maybe for financial reasons. When we apply eyelash extensions to a beauty guest, we have removers that were specifically for the eyelash adhesives that we use for these professional services. Having someone come in from another place doing a removal service is a risk, because we don't really know what type of adhesive was used to apply these lashes. . There really is no guarantee that the remover that was used was going to work for that person's lashes if the glue that was used was something that was extremely hard to break down. Normally a removal service usually takes about 15 minutes to 20 minutes tops, and it is a service that does not require much effort on our part except to apply the product to the beauty guest's lashes where the extensions were attached. This allows the product to breakdown the adhesive and these lashes will just slide off as we are wiggling them off the natural lashes.

    This removal definitely took an extremely long time, and she unfortunately lost a lot of her natural lashes because the adhesive or glue which was used was not supposed to be something to be used on the eyes. The services took probably an hour and fifteen, and thirty minutes to remove those lashes. Just like I stated, we are not pulling anything off, we were just applying the remover to the lashes and allowing that product to breakdown that adhesive or that bond. When we used our microfiber brushes to gently tap on the lashes, they would just come sliding off when they are ready to be removed. The glue that was used on this young lady pulled a lot of her lashes off, because they were bound in that thick heap of glue. This problem is why a cluster of lashes cannot be used for the same purposes of applying true individual lashes.

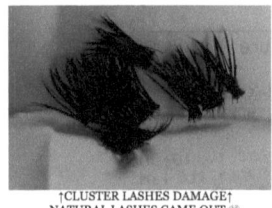
↑CLUSTER LASHES DAMAGE↑
NATURAL LASHES CAME OUT

These lashes have a purpose, but they were never meant to be worn on a long term basis. They were never meant to be used with semi-permanent extensions, adhesives or hair extensions or nail bonding glue. When I started doing eyelash extension years ago, I had to educate people about it. I had to let people know what cluster lashes really were, and that they were not individual eyelash extensions. It definitely was not easy. It took a lot of time. It took a lot of patience for me to continue to educate people about what these lashes were meant for and that what I specialized in was not the same as cluster lashes. So when someone said to me, "Oh I've received individual lashes before."

The Eyes Have It

I would literally ask them, "Okay, so what do these individual lashes look like?" As soon as they told me, I said there is no truth in what someone is selling you when they say that cluster lashes are the same as individual lashes. Yes, they are not an eyelash strip, but they are not individual eyelash extensions either. If someone is providing an eyelash service and they are only charging you $10-$20, you cannot compare it to what I am doing because it's just not the same thing! Higher quality products; true natural look and feel.

As I started seeing more and more of these over the years, I wanted to do something to help these women that were used to that look and also used to paying a lower price for these lashes. So I started offering cluster lashes in my business. What I was doing was so different from what these nail salons were doing or what some people or other places are doing when they are applying cluster lashes to their beauty guests. I would go through the process of making sure that my beauty guest's eyes were clean and their lashes are cleansed and oil free. I would have the

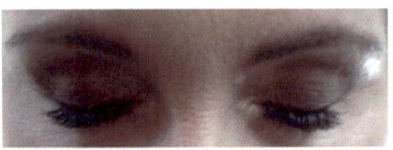

CLUSTER LASHES
DONE TO PERFECTION 👌

beauty guest lay down on the treatment table. I would cover their lower lashes as opposed to what these other places were doing with beauty guests sitting up on a chair and holding a fan while they were applying those lashes. I would use sensitive adhesives to apply the lashes to their natural lashes, and do it in a way that those lashes were not thick and heavy, but they would enhance their eyes and their look.

I have had a number of women that have this service done, and I've also educated them on the difference of cluster lashes and individual eyelash extensions. Thankfully a number of them have transitioned to getting individual eyelash extensions, because they saw the worth in what the difference was and they wanted something that was more semi-permanent and more natural looking and feeling.

The Eyes Have It

So eventually I stopped providing the cluster lashes in my beauty business, because it wasn't where my heart was. Honestly for those who had seen the difference, semi-permanent options were more ideal.

But for me, my mission was a lot bigger than just the look of their lashes but also about the health of their lashes. I wanted to ensure that what I was doing was not damaging to their lashes or their eyes in any way. I can thankfully say that is what exactly what I did. I have had so many people with these thick clumps of cluster lashes which were so heavy that it was made to look like an eyelash strip. It was just damaging to the beauty guests' lashes, and it really does not make sense that someone would do this to a beauty guest and allow them to walk away. If the lashes were damaged, then not only have you as a professional lost a client, but the beauty guest is going to damage your reputation as a 'Professional.'

Elizabeth Jennings

Not everything is about money. You have to care about your beauty guest's eyes, their lashes and the health of their lashes for the long term. So cluster lashes I do feel are the knock off of individual eyelash extensions, but they do serve a purpose when used and worn the right way. They are made for a temporary look.

They are made for enhancing a woman's lashes for a special occasion or event. They are not made to be worn like an individual eyelash extension with semi-permanent adhesives. I just simply believe that when you know better, you do better.

Chapter 5

Single Strand Eyelash Extensions - The True Individual Extension

Eyelash Extensions Revolutionize the Beauty Industry

Now this is what I am talking about! This is what I came for! Individual eyelash extensions are what I believe has really revolutionized the beauty industry. Yes, we've always had hair services and always had nail services. We've always had make up services to help to enhance the beauty of women (and men). But individual eyelash extensions have changed the game of beauty! Individual eyelash extensions actually originated in Asia and the eyelashes are made of synthetic fibers to emulate the look of a natural eyelash.

What individual lashes can do for the eyes and the awakening of the face is just marvelous! It can't even be explained in words because a picture is worth a thousand words.

Elizabeth Jennings

When I did my first set of eyelash extensions in 2008, I was extremely mesmerized by what it did for the eyes and the face of a woman. Individual eyelash come in different lengths, curvatures and even in different materials, ranging from synthetic to mink. They can be extremely short or they can be exaggeratedly long.

No matter how you scratch the surface, eyelash extensions just can really transform the look of a woman and take them from "0 to 100" in a matter of an hour or more. Performing the artistry of eyelash extensions over and over again has never become old or boring for me, because each and every time it is an amazing feature to have someone go from drab to fab. Even when they're coming in for a maintenance service, they are so thankful that I've gotten them back to what they were when they initially got their lashes done. There's nothing like it!

The Eyes Have It

How an Eyelash Curl Makes the Difference

My favorite eyelash curl has to be the D curl. D curl is a really nice exaggerated type curl and it just helps to give someone; who has either completely straight lashes or a slight natural curl, a nice uplifted eye appearance. The B curl eyelashes is great for someone that doesn't want too much, and they are not one who is commonly curling their lashes and their natural lashes are more relaxed to begin with. So the B curl has a nice relaxed curl, but it is still a pretty curl nonetheless. I will have to say that the most popular curl that we offer for our beauty guests are the C curl eyelashes. It is that middle range curl-extremely pretty while not being too much and still looking very natural. I tell you that one of the fun things that I have loved to do for many of my beauty guests is to mix the curls of extensions that I apply on them.

There are many beauty guests that I would use a B curl and a C curl on to blend those lashes together using the C curl on their lower layer of natural lashes so when their eyes are open the curl is more lifted. I would then use the B curl eyelashes on the top layer, so when their eyes are closed the curl looks a little more relaxed but again it's still beautiful and it blends perfectly. The single strand eyelash extensions are definitely what the true individual eyelash extension is. The beauty of the individual/single eyelash extension is that you can mix and match the curls to help each individual person.

This individual eyelash extension is applied to an isolated natural lash and not on the skin but about 2mm above the lash line so that when a full set is created, one has a really nice defined and full set of eyelash extensions and nothing is clumped together. One of the things I love hearing the most from beauty guests is when they say someone has noticed their lashes and say to them, "What type of mascara do you wear?" That is the best compliment ever!

The Eyes Have It

The idea of wearing individual eyelash extensions has dismissed that necessity of wearing any mascara on a regular basis, and also helps the beauty guest to continue to look extremely natural. No one's coming up to them and saying, "Oh my, you have on fake lashes!" That is what this investment is all about!

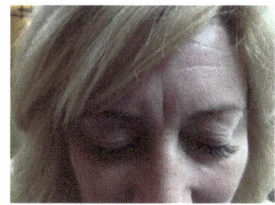 You would never be able to achieve that same effect with cluster lashes or eyelash strips, because they definitely look like you have put some false lashes on, even if they look decent. There's just no doubt about that. But with eyelash extensions; true individual eyelash extensions, you're going to get that natural effect.

Over the years, this has been one of the things that I definitely have to explain to people that would inquire about the service. They would say, "I don't want to look fake." My response to them would be, "There is no way I can make these lashes look fake, because they're made to replicate the look of a natural lash and they still have a natural look and a natural feel."

Elizabeth Jennings

Why Quality is Important

    I will never forget, that one of the best experiences that I ever had was back in 2009. At this point, I was working out of a new salon and spa; renting a space. I had a new beauty guest who came in, and she had lashes on already and was scheduled for an eyelash fill-in (or maintenance) appointment. When she came in and I brought her to the treatment room, she immediately told me she didn't know exactly why she needed a maintenance appointment. She just scheduled a fill-in, because she already had lashes on and she had gotten them done in another place about 2 weeks prior. She said she liked the thought of having lashes on but she didn't know if they were done properly, because they felt a little bit uncomfortable but she would trust my judgment. So I just told her honestly after examining her lashes; while she laid on the treatment table, that I didn't feel like I would be doing her any justice if I were to try and fill in her lashes because those extensions were clumped together.

The Eyes Have It

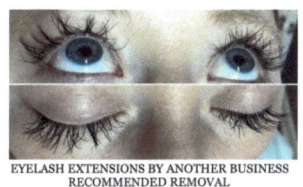
EYELASH EXTENSIONS BY ANOTHER BUSINESS RECOMMENDED REMOVAL

There was not a lot of care involved in applying the eyelash extensions, so a lot of them were not uniform, going in different directions, glued together, stuck and could very well have damaged her lashes if she allowed them to stay that way. So what I recommended was that we do a full removal and do a fresh full set of eyelash extensions; just starting over. She said that was fine, so that's what we did. She trusted my judgment and that was a great thing. (It really is an honor when a beauty guest trusts my professional judgment, because this truly is what I do!) It is true that most people do trust the service provider's judgment, but we all know that there are some people that are extremely demanding and they want what they want, when they want it and that is a hard place to be in. Sometimes you know that what they may want may not be what's best for them. I knew at that time doing a fill in was not going to be the best option for her; more importantly, pretty much impossible because of how clumped those lashes were in the first place.

So I went through with the removal and started fresh with the full set. When I was finished, I gave her the mirror. She dropped the mirror, turned around and gave me a big hug! I honestly was a bit stunned, but I accepted it with grace and honor and it almost made me cry! When she said to me, "I don't even feel them. I didn't know that I was not supposed to feel them, because I felt what I had 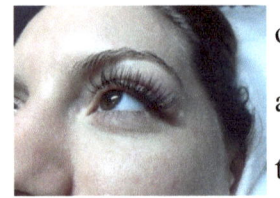 on before. These, I cannot feel them at all and they look beautiful!" Her gratitude was amazing. This show of appreciation is just one of the reasons that I do what I do. This appointment made her one of my regular beauty guests for many, many years after.

For single strand eyelash extensions, you have to apply them with definite care and intentional placement in order to provide a quality service and not have a beauty guest's lashes clumped together, sticky and feeling heavy or even hurting their eyes.

The Eyes Have It

I've worked with many women from many walks of life to provide this beauty service of individual eyelashes and it has been an honor for me, but sometimes it has been heartbreaking as well. I remember an instance when a beauty guest was scheduled to come in for fill in while she was in town for the weekend. I squeezed her in when I really didn't have the time to see her. I made it work because she really wanted to come in and get her eyelashes touched up, because she was going to be leaving the next day. So I got her in for the service. Now there are a lot of places that will not even provide a fill-in for a beauty guest that was not seen by that business before, but I don't ever want to turn someone away if I can help them. You really don't know what you have to deal with until that beauty guest comes in and you see what's going on. So when she came in for her appointment for eyelashes, what she had was really clumped together. When the beauty guest comes in for a fill-in, we want to cleanse the eyes and eyelashes with their eyes closed, and prep the lashes with primer which removes any embedded dirt oils or debris that may have been missed during the general cleansing. After this, we then go through the lashes by grooming and removing any lashes that are still hanging on but have grown out over 50% or more. We do this as carefully and quickly as possible. That's why we request beauty guests come in for their appointments without any makeup on; especially mascara as it slows down the process, because we want to start with a completely clean base. When a beauty guest is wearing makeup, it requires more cleaning than usual. Then we are fill in with extensions to the natural lashes.

    As soon as I saw the condition of her lashes, I told her that it was going to be difficult for me to fill in around what she had and I didn't want to charge her for a full set. I also told her that I would do the best that I could for her and her lashes. I was honest with her. As a lash artist with integrity, it wasn't about getting a quick buck but it was important to ensure her I would be giving her the best I was able to provide.

The Eyes Have It

She also thanked me and said that she appreciated my honesty and professional opinion. Now as I was working with her, I asked her how long she had been getting her eyelashes done. She had getting them done for a couple of years. Where she was located, there weren't many places

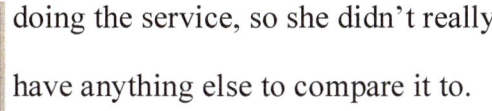

doing the service, so she didn't really have anything else to compare it to.

At this moment as I was going through her remaining eyelash extensions, I told her that it really was going to be quite difficult for me to provide a quality service for her like I normally do because of what was already on her eyes. I told her I would have to remove some of the lashes, but I will do the best that I can to provide a quality beauty service for her since I wasn't doing a full set for her that day. I removed some of her lash extensions that I could. I did the best with what time I had scheduled with her. Also as I was talking to her, I was educating her on what I felt her lashes looked like.

She stated that she felt her lashes were "okay" when she first received them, but she didn't know if the quality was the same as when she initially got them done. She also stated the service provider wasn't really doing many eyelash extensions services anymore, and that she was mainly focusing on other services that the med spa was offering where she was located.

I told her it could definitely be that the service provider was too busy and not focused on doing great lashes. I wanted to try to help her out as best as I was able to, and hoped she would be happy with the scheduled service I was providing her that day. When I gave her the mirror after completion, she was extremely happy and satisfied, and I'm glad that she was! I wasn't extremely happy with the quality of what I was able to do for her. I would have simply preferred to do a complete removal and a full set for her that day instead of trying to fill in around some work that was not the best quality. But sometimes we just have to do what we have to do. In that space and time, it is what worked for the beauty guest, and she was appreciative of it. It breaks my heart when I see something like that. Because when someone is doing an eyelash extensions service, I believe they have to really have the passion for providing this beauty service. There's just no way around that.

Why Passion and Patience Are Important

The art of eyelash extensions performance really takes a patient eye, a patient and steady hand, passion, character and integrity in order to give a really quality service. If someone is not passionate about it and they're just simply doing it for the money, they can really just fly through the service and do a unsatisfactory job; quite frankly that angers me! I hate to see people do things like that. I would never do that to anyone. As an eyelash specialist, we're isolating a beauty guest's natural lash one by one in order to place an extension on that lash in the proper way. When that is not being done you're doing yourself; as the service provider and the beauty guest, a disservice! Who wants to continue to go to a service provider that does a rushed sloppy work? I know I don't, and neither do many beauty guests either. They may put up with it for a little while if they do not know any better; but after a while, they will definitely get the hint and cease to get their service done. I believe that is what sets myself apart as a Master Lash Artist compared to others who just do eyelash extensions as a service on their menu. I am truly passionate about lashes, and I ensure that the team that works in my beauty business is really the same way! You not only have to know how to do the service exceptionally well, you have to love it as well! How many 'companies' require a love for what you will be doing? Not many; but if more did, they would probably have less problems with less turnovers, don't you think? I have had a few come and go in my beauty business; but honestly, it mainly was for this same reason, and I just can't have anyone that isn't really enjoying what they do with our beauty guests.

The Eyes Have It

Becoming an eyelash specialist so many years ago, was really almost a foreign concept in my community. Not many people really understood the intricacies of my job. The first thing I had to do was start an education campaign. Education! Educating the masses about what I was offering, was definitely no walk in the park to get to people to realize how tedious the service was but also to know how worthy the investment really was. There were so many places doing the cluster lashes, and were indeed calling those lashes individual eyelashes. I had to educate a lot of customers/beauty guests about the difference in what I was doing as opposed to what the others were doing.

When an individual eyelash extension is done, the beauty guest is lying down on the treatment table and kept in a relaxed zone. Their lower lashes are covered and their eyes are completely closed. I have to use specialized tools and specialized eyelash extension tweezers to isolate one individual natural lash using tweezers in my left hand

and then using tweezers in my right hand to pick up an individual eyelash. I dip that individual eyelash that I've picked up into adhesive making sure the adhesive is on the individual eyelash in the proper way. I then have to place that on the natural lash that I have isolated, and doing all of these simultaneously while not having anything applied to the skin. (Try doing all of that without breathing! I've definitely held my breath a time or two LOL!)

That is not one of the easiest things to do. I had to really inform and educate the public that this is no different than any cosmetic plastic surgery procedure where you would want to come in for a consultation, go over the different options and see what is going to suit you best. You don't just walk into a plastic surgeon's office and say, "I want a breast enhancement." You have to go through a process, and you have to ensure that you are a good candidate for the service or the procedure that you are inquiring about.

Chapter 6

Russian Volume Lashes

The Answer to Our Voluminous Prayers

The Power of Advertising

When you look at commercials for mascara ads and you see the pictures and the videos of the models or celebrities that are in these commercials, the one thing that we cannot deny is the fullness and the depth and darkness of their eyelash area. There are a few reasons for that. The first being, that the creators of mascara knew that when someone was using the product, it is really because they wanted to make their lashes more intensified and make them look fuller.

The second reason those models and celebrities' lashes looks so full in these commercials, is because it's rarely the mascara product that is giving them that darker and fullness intensity. It is more often than not because the model or celebrity has had lashes applied or the lashes are digitally enhanced.

Now that idea may sound crazy to some, but if you look at the next mascara commercial; read the fine print. More people don't see this, because they're focusing on the product and the model that is in this commercial! It's honestly something I never really recognized before or paid attention to before becoming a lash stylist.

Over the years as I have been able to provide the service to many beauty guests, the number one question that would be asked of me after a beauty guest has gotten their lashes done for a short or maybe over a longer period of time is – "Is there any way we can apply more lashes?" When eyelash extensions are applied, we're applying one individual eyelash extension to one individual natural lash. We can do this to the extent of the fullness of the beauty guest's lashes. If the beauty guest has very sparse lashes, there's only so much that we can do. Even if the beauty guest has very dense lashes, we can only apply as much extensions as they have natural lashes.

The Eyes Have It

We try to not apply extensions to the very outer corner or the very inner corner lashes, because these lashes are much thinner and they tend to either droop down or they point towards the outer ear (the outer corner lashes) or the bridge of the nose (the inner corner lashes). Applying lashes to those areas would not be ideal so we tend to skip those areas. We also want to not apply individual eyelash extensions to the very fresh new growth eyelashes that are coming in, because they're just not strong enough to hold the extension yet. These lashes are more weaker, very fragile and they need more time to grow.

We need to give those lashes a little more time to grow and be stronger before applying an extension to those lashes. So over the years, one of my dilemmas was when I would have a beauty guest that did not have really full natural lashes in the beginning who would want more than I could offer to them.

Elizabeth Jennings

A Miracle Called Russian Volume Lashes

But in late 2012, I learned about 'Russian Volume Lashes.' The technique of Russian Volume Lashes is simply nothing but amazing! With lashes that are made very thin, we are able to apply more than one extension to a natural lash in variations of two dimensional - all the way up to 7 dimensional! We're not just simply grabbing lashes and placing them on, there's a method and a science to doing so. The lashes are applied fluffy and full and not looking as if we just applied a lot of clusters of lashes onto a beauty guest. There is a significant difference between Russian volume lashes, cluster lashes and even individual eyelash extensions.

This goes far beyond those early strips, cluster lashes or individual eyelash extensions lash techniques and styles. This technique was one of the first times that I began to truly feel like I could give my beauty guests exactly what they desired and deserved.

The Eyes Have It

I got my first training for volume lash extensions in late 2013 and have had four trainings, four professional trainings in volume lash extensions, and I learn something very different each and every time. But all in all, what I gained from these professional trainings was the ability to give the beauty guests the density that many were asking about

for years from receiving the individual eyelash extensions.

One of the things I have hated most about my job is the fact that I've had to say to numerous beauty guests, "This is the fullest that your lashes will get because of how sparse your lashes are." Of course anything other than just mascara giving them more fullness and length than they had before, but they were seeking more and Russian volume lashes was the "more" that they were looking for. It was the eyelash holy grail. Volume lashes are primarily focused on increasing the fullness and not so much in extending the length of the lashes. The shorter the lashes tend to be, the fuller they will appear.

When we go with using much longer lashes; yes they may be more fullness, but they will not look as dense as they would appear if we were to go with shorter eyelashes.

One of my beauty guests was in her early 60s. She had been a beauty guest for several years, and she was getting the individual eyelash extensions. They did a world of difference for her, but her natural lashes were extremely sparse and very thin. When I told her about the volume lash extensions, that was right after her father had passed away. She had personally been through a lot with the death of her father, his extended sickness, wrapping up his estate and needed to really start doing more things for herself. We scheduled an appointment for her to get the volume lash extensions. She went with 2D or two dimensional volume lashes.

So I did a full removal of her lashes, and then we went with the full set of 2D volume lashes. I tell you that when she looked in that mirror, she was stunned!

The Eyes Have It

Now I never received a text message from her during the time I was working with her, but that next day; it was a Sunday, she sent me a text message and said simply, "I love my lashes!" That warmed my heart so much, because of the fact that she took the time to send me a text message; something that she never did before, the very next day just to let me know how much she loved her lashes. I hit the bullseye for her! (Another Score for the Master Lash Artist!)

I was right on target with what she was looking for after so many years. Though she was always pleased with the service that she was receiving and with the eyelash extensions that she was getting, this truly was the icing on the cake for her. Volume lashes are really the icing on the cake for so many of my beauty guests. The majority of the beauty guests who I worked with to this very day all have volume lash extensions, and many of them wore individual eyelash extensions before this time.

Many of my clients/beauty guests have transitioned into wearing volume lash extensions, and many of those same people have never looked back. I've had a couple of people that had transitioned back from wearing volume lashes to the individual eyelash extensions, but it was primarily for work reasons; nothing other than that.

Different Dimensional Volume Lashes

Whether one decides to get two dimensional (2D) volume lashes, three dimensional (3D) volume lashes, all 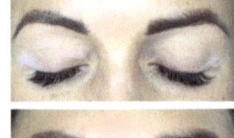 the way up to seven dimensional (7D); it's hard for them to look fake. As you now understand, the D stands for dimensional and the number applies to the number of extensions that adhere to one natural lash. I would have to say 3D has been the most popular choice for many of the beauty guests that I have worked with, but I am one that wears 4D or four dimensional volume lashes myself. I absolutely love the look of them, and I love to go with the D curl and shorter extensions for myself.

The Eyes Have It

Volume lashes is definitely a work of beauty art, and it can take anywhere from three or more hours to ap-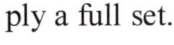ply a full set.

Both the client and the service provider must have patience in order to get the right extensions.

But I don't mind. I absolutely love doing volume lashes, and I am always in the zone when I am creating a full set from the beginning or when I am recreating a full set when a beauty guest comes in for their fill-in appointment. Though there are more than one extension that is applied to the natural lash, this technique is completely safe because the extensions are very thin. When a beauty guest comes in, we would never want to recommend anything that would be too much for that individual beauty guest. I have a number of beauty guests who are older and have volume lashes applied regularly.

Elizabeth Jennings

I definitely would not commonly recommend to them that they go with something in the four dimensional or upper categories of Volume Lashes, because it would be just a bit too much for their natural lashes to be able to handle.

This really helps to fill in the sparseness or spaces that some beauty guests have, and it's not about the price but it is about the quality that I would want my beauty guest to have. I never want to sell anyone short of what I believe their potential could be, based on the look that they are going for. I have had the opportunity to train everyone on my beauty team in this technique over the past few years, and it has been an amazing experience. For some, it has been extremely intimidating because it is not the easiest technique to perform. Being able to create this voluminous work of art, gives the team such pride when the beauty guest looks in the mirror and says, "My eyes look amazing!"

The Eyes Have It

One of the girls on my beauty team does the lashes of an incredible hair stylist who works at a salon. She absolutely loves the work that we do and the work her service provider does personally for her.

She came into my beauty room one day with the beauty guest just to show off her lashes, and she was so in love with the look!

She has even stated how she brags about her lashes so much that she wanted us to be a part of their one year hair salon celebration, and that truly was an honor. It is always an honor when someone wants to recommend you to someone else. It is an extreme honor to have someone who is in the same industry; that may not be doing exactly the same services that you are doing, wants to be able to let others know about the service that they are receiving at another beauty business.

Elizabeth Jennings

How awesome is that?! So volume lashes definitely have been a hit and will continue to remain a hit as far as I am concerned and believe. Volume is here to stay!

Chapter 7

From Subtle to Sexy - Why A "Little" is Never Enough

So in the very beginning of my eyelash artist career, it was always about enhancing the look but not taking away from the look. Many times when I was doing eyelash extensions in the very beginning, I was always trying to be extremely conservative because where I'm located it is a pretty conservative area. I never wanted to take away from a woman's look, but I only wanted to enhance what they naturally already have. Every time I would begin a consultation with a new beauty guest, I always wanted to reassure them that eyelash extensions are made to look natural. I shared this, because I felt it was important for a beauty guest not to go too far with the look and the length or the fullness of the set that they would choose. I also would get questions from beauty guests about the lashes; because let's face it, in society we tend to see a number of 'bad lash jobs.'
I had to train myself not to look at people that had those

really thick lashes with the goopy thick glue which looked so heavy that their eyelids were hard to open. I tried my best to keep a straight face when I would see this! Since I have worked for many years with many beauty guests, I understand that women are looking to enhance their looks while being secure in the fact that I'm not going to make them look 'overly fake.' Some refer to the 'overly fake' as

 the 'drag queen' look. This became an easier feature to accomplish with eyelash extensions, because they do look and feel so natural; it's like you're not wearing anything at all. It was actually quite common for someone to go from an extremely conservative look to inquiring and requesting something with more fullness and a little more boldness. As I have lashed more and more beauty guests, I have become accustomed to having the request to add more lashes time and time again!

This request would come from those who wanted the more subtle looks for their lashes at first.

The Eyes Have It

I even became more of a fan of the fuller sets of lashes on myself, so I definitely understood it and could relate.

Subtlety is great, but so is sexiness! There is not one type of lash which is better than another, but it's just a preference for an individual person. When one is extremely conservative and they want to keep it subtle, I always recommended that we start slow. I would recommend we start with the minimum and then as we go along with the maintenance and fill-in appointments, we could always add a little bit more by adding them steadily and slowly as we progress. I wouldn't suggest someone that is on the more conservative side starting with for instance about 45 individual eyelash extensions on each eye to bumping up to 125 lashes at the very next appointment. That may be too much of a shock for their beautiful system! If we add about 20 lashes each time they come in to that initial set, that definitely will be a subtle change in the fullness; not anything too drastic where it would cause them to feel as if they needed to have any eyelashes that were applied removed immediately.

Elizabeth Jennings

There are some who can take it, and there is no fear in a drastic change. I have had a beauty guest who decided to change from a very subtle set of individual eyelash extensions to an extremely full set of individual eyelash extensions.

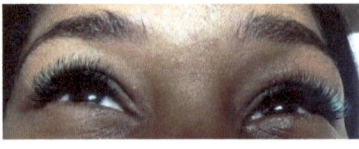

I have even had beauty guests who have come in for a temporary set of eyelashes just to try it out for an event, to realize how much they loved having lashes on and decide to go into a full set of Russian volume lashes! That definitely is a huge change! There is nothing wrong with going from subtle to sexy for an eyelash look. Either way, they all are going to be simply gorgeous! Admittedly, growing up in and living in such a conservative place really was a risk for me to go into something that was as groundbreaking as performing the beautiful art of eyelash extensions.

The Eyes Have It

With the differences in the lengths, the curls and diameters of eyelashes, there are also differences in the colors available.

Eyelash extensions come in all of the colors of the rainbow and then some! It hasn't been an extremely popular service here, but I must say the opportunities that I have had to apply colored lashes to individuals has been nothing short of a blast of excitement for me! I am a lover of color lashes on myself as well, because it does really give the eye an accentuation and appeal that regular black or brown eyelash extensions just don't do.

Purple eyelash extensions have been my color of choice and it is just one of my favorite colors, but it tends to be the one that I gravitate towards most when it comes to my personal lashes. The color purple really helps my brown eyes pop, and I get so many compliments on them when I am outdoors in the sunlight.

Elizabeth Jennings

Once I was in Arizona for a business conference and there were hundreds of people in attendance.

The question that I was asked the most as I was meeting attendees was, "Do you have purple eyelashes on?" and "Wow, those look beautiful!" So the idea of colored lash extensions is definitely is a conversation starter.

For several years, color lashes were something that I did not promote, and I rarely asked beauty guests if they were interested in. So when I had the first beauty guest ever that outright requested to have color lashes, it was a great moment for me and this beautiful beauty guest has been coming for years. She continues to get her purple eyelash extensions added to her lash line. There was a beauty guest years ago that got a full set of eyelash extensions, and she was really hesitant about them being noticeable at all.

The Eyes Have It

When we are normally applying a set of eyelash extensions, we don't go much longer in length than the beauty guest's longest natural eyelash as not to take away from what the beauty guest already has. We don't want their lashes to be the very first thing that people mention; we must be careful to make it not obvious that extensions were applied. We did a full set of lashes for this beauty guest, and they looked really natural but she didn't want 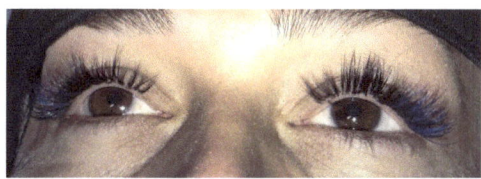 them to be noticeable at all! I had to explain to her that she was getting a full set of eyelashes so they are going to be noticeable, but they are not going to look fake. So what I suggested that we do for her; which is something that I have never suggested for anyone before, was to go with a half set of lashes and actually go shorter in length for the eyelash extensions that we were using on her full set.

Elizabeth Jennings

This was a rare instance, but it happened. And when we went with the suggestion, she was definitely pleased. For some, the idea of being completely subtle is the major requirement for the lash extension.

For many others, being as bold and sexy as they possibly can with their eyelashes is just what they have realized they desired and required.

The Eyes Have It

Chapter 8

It's Not For Everyone, But For the Majority… Lashes RULE!!!

Being a master lash artist, I tend to feel like eyelash extensions can solve many of life's problems and can answer a lot of unfulfilled questions in life. That may sound "ridiculous;" but honestly, there is a lot that lash extensions can do for a person. In the beauty art of eyelash extensions, one of the main ingredients that is required in order to do the service appropriately, is the eyelash extensions' adhesive.

In life, people can build up an allergy towards many things at any time. Some people are allergic to latex. Some people are allergic to detergents, perfumes, and many other things. The amount of allergens these days has skyrocketed. I do not know the reason for this, but it is a fact. With that being said, some people have developed an allergy to the ingredient that may be in eyelash extensions adhesive.

Even though this product is not touching the skin that doesn't really matter at all. There have been people that have had an allergic reaction to eyelash extensions and have not been able to wear them.

This is not something that happens often, but unfortunately has occurred. This is why we would highly recommend a beauty guest who has experienced allergies of some sort, or who have higher tendencies towards sensitivities, come in for a patch test. A patch test involves the service provider applying a few lashes to the potential beauty guest's lashes. So for those who have developed an allergy of course, eyelash extensions are unfortunately are not for them. Some people have had no problems wearing eyelash extensions and then over time they have developed an allergy.

The Eyes Have It

There are others who have just been outright sensitive to many things and it never was something that they were able to tolerate in the first place. For the patch test, what we would do is apply a couple of extensions to each eye on the natural lashes; nothing on the skin.

Over the 24 to 48-hour period, they can see how their eyes tolerate the lashes that were applied. If they do not tend to have any issues, then what we would suggest is scheduling the full set of eyelash extensions to be applied. For many, this has worked out extremely well.

There are sensitive eyelash adhesives. But unfortunately a lot of the main ingredients that are required to hold up to the elements and things that could cause the breakdown of the adhesive in between appointments, are not in the sensitive adhesives. Because these sensitive adhesives are not as strong, the eyelash extensions do not hold up as well in between fill-ins, and they tend to start shedding off of the natural lashes within a week or less sometimes.

For those reasons, I tend to not even recommend eyelash extensions for those people that have sensitivities but would want to try getting eyelash extensions anyway with a sensitive adhesive. Honestly, it's not going to work well in their favor, and I just believe that it would be a waste of time and money for everybody involved. Then of course there are other medical issues that would be a contra-indication to one that would want to wear eyelash extensions.

This condition; Trichotillomania, involves a nerve or nervous reaction that causes the beauty guest to pull out their hair; whether it is their eyebrow hair, their eyelash hair or their hair on the scalp. I have had a number of potential beauty guests in the past that have known themselves to have this condition. They would call in and ask if this service would be something that I would recommend to help them not do this anymore.

I would never mislead anyone, and I would always let them know that unfortunately I do not recommend wearing eyelash extensions if they have this condition, because it is not going to stop them from pulling out their hair.

Then there's 'Alopecia.' Alopecia is another medical condition. It is not exactly known what causes it or why someone has alopecia, but it is a known fact that stress can exacerbate alopecia symptoms. Alopecia means that the hair is simply falling out - sometimes the hair grows back and sometimes it does not. Sometimes when the hair does grow back, it grows back very thin and fine. For these sufferers, I do not recommend wearing eyelash extensions either. I would of course love to help all these people out in some way with eyelash extensions. I just love the service so much, that I feel like it's done so much good for so many people. But unfortunately for them, it's just not something that I would recommend. I would recommend a natural set of eyelash strips for someone with this condition for a temporary occasional wear.

Elizabeth Jennings

Then of course, there are people that simply the service is not for. And that's okay! I can remember a time when I received a call from a woman that was inquiring about getting the service done. She told me that someone she knew once came in to get the eyelash extensions at my beauty business before. She spoke very highly of the business and all of those things that went along with the service that she received, but she said that she could not get used to wearing the eyelashes because it wasn't something she had ever done before. She just could not stop pulling on her eyelashes and rubbing her eyes. So the prospective beauty guest was asking me if this was normal and if this was something that I dealt with on a regular basis. I had to tell her that this was absolutely not something that I was use to hearing anyone do, nor that was something that many people did because it simply was not the case. I just had to inform her and be extremely honest with her upfront, that if this person that she spoke to was speaking about the service that way, it's just simply because it wasn't the service that was for her.

The Eyes Have It

Not everything is for everybody. I don't get my nails done, they drive me crazy! It's just not what I do, but I don't knock the service.

I realize that it is not something I can get done for myself; although, I think nails and nail designs are absolutely beautiful!

The many thousands of women that I have had the experience of working with over the years to provide this amazing beauty transformative art. I can't say that any of them ever said anything in the slightest about their eyelash extensions. What I hear on a regular basis; especially from my beauty guests who come in over and over again for their maintenance is that, "I'm back!" "I feel that I'm alive again!" "Oh my God, I could not wait to see you I've been waiting to get my lashes done!" and the list continues. These are the things that I hear more common than I hear a complaint about eyelash extensions.

Elizabeth Jennings

So just like everything isn't for everybody, eyelash extensions are not for everybody. (Although I'm a bit biased and believe they should be, eyelash extensions may not be for everyone, but definitely for the majority eyelashes rule!)

The service that began primarily in Asian countries over ten years ago, is simply not going anywhere. Yes, there has been a lot of negative press about eyelash extensions. Sometimes reports or the media does not understand the infinite possibilities of lash extensions. Other times, there may be a hot topic after someone has had an unfortunate experience. That one bad experience gets a lot of media attention that may take the focus off of the many good experiences that happen regularly. When the service is done the right way (by someone who is educated and certified to do the correct service), it is rare that you would hear about a bad experience. When I hear the stories that some have shared with me that I have had the pleasure of providing beauty services for, it warms my heart.

The Eyes Have It

While sometimes there is user error (in terms of a beauty guest not following the instructions); most of the time, the eyelash extensions are done correctly and help the beauty guest with the desired enhancement.

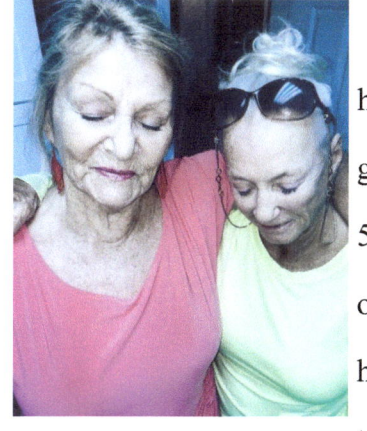

For example; when I had one of my precious beauty guests bring in a friend of over 50 years to treat her to a full set of eyelash extensions, I was honored! Her friend was just in town for the weekend, so she wasn't sure if she would keep them up. But the way she lit up when she looked in the mirror, there was no denying that was a beauty investment that was well worth it. So when she returned to her home state, she decided to go to an eyelash specialist not far from her home who could keep up the maintenance to the beautiful enhance she received. After losing her husband about a year prior, this was something that really helped to pick up her spirits and make her feel beautiful again.

Elizabeth Jennings

That is what it is all about for me; enhancing eyes and enhancing lives! I absolutely love lashes and what it has done for looks and also what is has done for my life.

It has helped to carve out the purpose for me to connect with so many amazing beauty guests, and enhance their natural beauty. I wouldn't have it any other way. I think of my career as not just a licensed aesthetician and a master lash artist, but a "people specialist," since I am helping all my beauty guests become the best 'extension' of themselves. I wouldn't have it any other way!

www.ingramcontent.com/pod-product-compliance
Lightning Source LLC
Chambersburg PA
CBHW042305150426
43197CB00001B/19